SallyGray is Gone

CSF Publishing
This edition copyright © 2021 CSF Publishing, USA
All poems © 2021 Joe De Patta
Introduction © 2021 John Biscello
Art cover © Sally Gray
Cover art: *Orange 1* by Sally Gray
Joe De Patta portrait © Katy Ballard

Paperback ISBN 978-1-7360311-4-8
Web: csfpublishing.com
E-mail: info@csfpublishing.com

All characters appearing in this work are fictitious. Any resemblance to real persons, living or dead, is purely coincidental.

No part of this book may be reproduced in any form or by any electronic or mechanical means, including information storage and retrieval systems, without written permission from the publisher or the author, except in the case of a reviewer, who may quote brief passages embodied in critical articles or in a review.

To the loving memory of Sally Gray. Artist, Poet. Everything.

SallyGray is Gone

Joe De Patta

CSF Publishing

"Why so much fear of tears? Because the masks we use are made of salt. A stinging, red salt which makes us beautiful and majestic but devours our skin."

Luisa Valenzuela

Introduction

Let us imagine a concert of poems as a masquerade party. At the party, revelry and spite commingle like embolic teenagers. Dancing takes place on the veranda of lost hours. The moonlight occasionally shines upon incidents of scarring and disfigurement, which are seamlessly woven into the masks. So many masks, each serving a function and purpose, as if repertory stock options from a Noh drama that lives somewhere between rehearsal and performance. The masks consort as an assembly of tensions and counterpoints—rubbing noses, parroting vowels, grazing lips, delegating primacy . . . They become the pronouns through which lives are given design and order. There's also kissing. Lots of kissing, and inveterate gestures that keeps the party moving, and true to the spirit of communion. Or showmanship. Sometimes you can't tell the two apart.

Joe De Patta's debut poetry collection is such a party, one with a pinwheeling spectrum of moods, tones and themes that finds light by caving in on itself, and then funneling outward through the dignity of cracks.

In this collection, you will meet a man, and his cadre of masks, plumbing between the lines, sometimes with acidic furor and seething, sometimes with clipped wistfulness; always with a marksman's sense of dark comedy and inbred romanticism. Think Baudelaire cross-bred with George Carlin, wielding a bouquet of Molotov cocktails ... just in case. This is poetry, same as it is a stand-up routine delivered in one of Dante's after-hour clubs in the red-light district.

De Patta takes you through the benumbing vacuum of consumerism, where customers become comic-strip obituaries in the aisles of Wal-Mart. He takes you into the religious armpit of a Catholic-Italian childhood. Takes you into a garage where the helium-inflated dreams of rock n' roll stardom are born, begrudgingly grow older, find themselves crippled, shoot up, swallow pills, have affairs, grow middle-aged and paunchy, wonder about wrong turns and emergency exits, grow older still, die tragic deaths, find themselves resurrected, and keep questing after the rock n' roll grail with quixotic aplomb. There is all of this, and there is a lot more, and then there is Sally Gray.

Sally Gray is the thinly veiled heartbeat of this collection, the sun in its carefully arranged solar system. You don't meet Sally Gray, at least not officially, until a bit later in the book, but the magnitude of her presence is there, from start to finish. Sometimes as silent company, other times as a bright star and inspiration, sometimes as the name which now covers a new territory of grief, other times as artist, confidante, and memory warmed over to the point of fever. She is there. And then again, she is not. And that is the emotional fulcrum of De Patta's collection.

We each live within concealed and elaborate systems of hair-sensitive trigger-points and habituations, a minefield of neuroses that are stalked through with equal measures of determination and fatigue. These rigged aggregations, and their multiple moving parts, often find themselves at the mercy of life's sideshow dealings. Are we engaged in a comedy of tragic errors, or is it a tragedy of comic errors, and what masks should we wear to these occasions? De Patta's poetry is the sifted grains of these philosophical meditations. He speaks of "bright punctuation to a dark hour," and he ambles through wreckage with a name carved into the tenderest bits of his heart, a talisman embedded in pulp. Sally Gray.

At one point in his poetic pilgrimage, a softly reflective De Patta muses, "I am different. Not better, but there is color." This book stands as an agitated testament to that, and to many other survivalist qualities that remain fiercely on the side of life.

John Biscello

Aisle 12

The parking lot is tangled with trucks, cracked windshields and bald tires. Lost souls look For lost vehicles. I feel as though I'm being watched. Walk carefully, no eye contact.

"Hi, welcome to Walmart."

Everything is here. Flashlights and bubble bath and candy and shoes,

Sodas and peanut butter, lingerie and booze.

Feature rich, inexpensive, assembled by a 12-year-old; all merchandise guaranteed to Wear out in six months.

With other shoppers I am alone. Families roam, confused. Nothing to do but eat.

There is a pharmacy. Firearms for sale.

When it all ends, I may be here, what better place than Walmart? Which way should I Turn when it all kicks off: Guns or Drugs?

So easy to get lost. There, in the distance, vanishing in a red vest with nametag. When I Get there, she's gone.

Lightbulbs. Computer paper. This is life.

The red vest again. I hustle, left, right, avoid a very old man with a panicked expression, Dry skin. He snorts.

There. The red vest, the name tag. Rita. Oh, Rita, "Where are the lightbulbs? Where is the computer paper?"

"Aisle 12. I think. Down that way, I think, past the plumbing supplies, one or two lanes over from fertilizer. Probably. I think."

This is life and I'm alive, so I turn and retrace my steps, past the old man who is now Openly crying and a family shares a giant bag of M&Ms.

Very bad signage. Poor directions, misspellings, and I'm at aisle 8 and I've run into

A solid wall of sunglasses.

There are no red vests now. Customers stare into the void, squint at labels. Forlorn, read The Nutritional information on a bag of crunchy extra hot bacon rinds.

I am weary. A woman glides, blind approach, she lies across the handle of her cart, her wheeled torso, loud bad breath.

If I had a shopping cart I, too, could fold my arms across it, reverently bow my head and rest, Perhaps to sleep, to dream, to run into something.

Ahoy! Another red vest. Dylan. "Computer Paper, Dylan! Light Bulbs! Where? I've been told Aisle 12, but there is no Aisle 12. Where did you get that vest?"

"I just started here. I'm training. I don't know my way around. Go back that way and look for Rita?"

If I sit on this dirty floor, snatch a rubberized bath mat, wrap it around my trembling Body, and shout madly, "Lightbulbs Computer Paper! You pricks," then, you bet Dylan And Rita would be there

In a snap, the fat woman half asleep on her shopping cart, head on flabby arms films the Aftermath.

Death. Posted on YouTube. The Walmart death of a lost man, life ends on Aisle 12.

There is no computer paper or light bulbs or Aisle 12. It's the last thing I know before the Final spasm.

Aisle 11: Automotive supplies. Tire repair kits, windshield wiper fluid, furry seat covers. Aisle 13: Candy colored children's toys, sleeping bags and panties.

There is no rescue. Clammy, short of breath and panicked, this is the way it will end. Curled up, coughing my last words, tearful and terrified. Afterlife is Walmart, I'll

Never find my car and there are no goddamn lightbulbs.

My Pledge

No hurry on a shaded rural road water runs in the ditches white cumulus clouds
　Set off The New Mexico blue sky

　I turned my wheel sharply and tried to hit a prairie dog as it ran
　　In front of the car
　　Froze
　　Stood upright (as they do)
　　Ran back to its starting point.
　　I missed
　　It wouldn't be the first, run over, run down, slain by vehicle
　　Later in the year dried and crusted
　　Carcasses punctuate the two lanes
　　All the way to town

　　But I question my reasoning
　　Not a dangerous creature, not a threat
　　Millions of them roam everywhere, a most non-endangered animal
　　Still, I tried to kill it
　　Smear it into the asphalt
　　Quick flat death
　　Before I veered at the creature I knew I would have to answer that question again,
　　　"What the hell is wrong with you?" Rhetorical
　　The assumption that there was indeed something wrong
　　The interrogation was less a query than an accusation
　　I knew,
　　As a child I knew they never expected an answer, which was terrific because I couldn't have one.

　What was wrong with me? No idea. In fact, I thought I was all right, normal, ordinary Like others
　　But so many years later, I missed the Prairie Dog by a breath a tire's width and asked
　　The question, still the same question. I thought I'd never hear it again

The question I've not been able to answer, the question
I've heard for decades
What is wrong with you?
Hell if I know. Perhaps nothing. Is there a need to kill that
resides
Tamped down, ignored, crushed and mashed
Tilted and twisted.
I pledge, I swear, I will try not to kill another Prairie Dog
for the remainder of the year Until they migrate underground
to
The burrows and live safely in the dark below the snow.
I swear I will not
So I won't have to ask that question of myself because
they are gone, the question Remains
Swerves into my path
There was never an answer
Once I said, "Because I'm bad?"
To give the impression I was listening.

Preheating the Oven

I'm waiting for the oven to heat up
To 500 degrees. For a chicken. A technique I learned From Bill,
Who died of cancer surprise two years ago.
He cooked
So do I
500 is hot as hell then turns it down to 350 for 20 minutes a pound
He had a pain in his left side great skier, hiker
The doctors said he should take medication for a pulled muscle in his ribs
Stretched too far and split the seams.

After a month he'd used up all his pain meds and went back
No relief No relief
So, of course, X-rays and imaging. He called the next day
"I've got melanoma," he giggled and I could hear the fear behind the offhand tone
Lung cancer for a guy who never smoked didn't drink ate perfect food exercised
Was never fat. He weighed 155 pounds, lean and wiry
The healthiest guy
We used to laugh how skinny he was
We talked on the phone and walked in the hills had lunch every Tuesday for years, dinner at home, errands, help when needed.
Ten years ago I was troubled
Frightened, ready to blow up a great life
Bill called I answered told him, "I can't leave the house. I can't go anywhere. If I do I'll buy a bottle of gin and I'll drink it and drive around and then it will be all over. I can't leave the house I know I can't, I'll cause more damage to everyone, and I can't leave the house."
Bill said, "You are not leaving the house. You are talking to me on the phone."
Brought me back, a friend on the line, real, good-humored, kind. I think of him whenever I cook a chicken. Not a bad legacy.

Poets, Writers, and Artists

Eat like a horse drink like a fish run like a deer cry like a baby swears like a sailor lie like a rug laugh like a loon
   Walleyed jughead lantern jaw hyperactive universal multitasking clown shoes tee-shirt sweat pants knuckled under knee jerking
   Finger pointing half-dead pie-faced nose bleed
   Loud drunk unwashed uncombed unkempt unambitious undisciplined unfriendly Unemployed often unconscious and inconsistent demanding and clumsy
   Here they are. Poets and writers and artists. (Look at them. Look at them.)
   Do you recognize the one you saw that night? The one who stole that lady's purse
   Who punched that man and took his watch
   That pushed the little kid to the ground
   And laughed as he ran away,
   The girl who smeared jam
   All over her face and tried to kiss yo

   The woman who took your picture without asking permission
   That one teacher who took off his shirt in class?

   The Poet who keeps calling and hangs up without leaving a message?

Nature Poem

I won't, can't write about nature
No one should write about nature
Percy Shelley and H. D. Thoreau
Spare me the nature poem
The air, the trees, the mountains,
Leave it alone,
OK, you took a walk, saw a wildflower, a rock
Recoiled at a snake
Made noise so you weren't bothered by bears
A great day
Didn't fall down, drown, you weren't attacked by toothy mammals
Or hikers
Lumberjacks' Mountain bikers
Farmers Hunters
Could you hold off describing the way you feel when you're Outside?
(Did you leave your phone in the car? No, no you didn't)
Please avoid a poem about a camping trip or
Your walk among the Aspens,
I can amble without metaphors,
How steep the climb, color of leaves,
The once-in-a-lifetime experience that others can never realize
(Nature poetry should be read to the housebound
Show them what they are missing)
Or take a photo (With your phone, because I know you have it with you) email it to
Your confined friends
Bedridden Jailed Hostages to a job
What is the name of that lake
That meadow
The expanse of mesa and those mountains
On the distant horizon? Did you have a spiritual experience, a vision, did you
See a flying saucer hovering above the peaks?
Was there a strange sound, voices
Did the, Oh God, did the wind speak to you? Do your po-

ems give a voice to the land and
Are you the voice of the unheard? What a wonderful thing. Tread carefully
Through the trees to the
Meadow
Just don't write about it, please.

Unless you see a flying saucer.

Every Rock Band in the World

Track 1. Bad Marriage (Metal)

They fade out, vaporize, decay to
The trembling echo of bands breaking up,
Reverberation of failed songs
("What key? What key?") There have been disappearances and accidents two suicides.
The drums are the heart, the bass the balls,
The back and arms for heavy lifting belong to rhythm guitar
The lead is the brain and it resembles the
Bad marriage of four people with their assorted infidelities and resentments
After two years they cannot stand it, argue, throw things
But continue to rehearse
Practice
Jam
See what happens
An idea for a new tune
They know more than they should about each other
Know that achieving the right music is painful,
Loud fast and sharp
If you don't hurt
If you aren't injured then you didn't play hard enough and you suck
Sore and tired, gritty and damp
Ready to fight, refuse to talk
Insecure, lonely, tense
Prepared to fight for your tempo
The eternal argument between drum and bass: You were speeding up
You were lagging
Behind
Are you drunk?
Are you stoned?
Coke makes you play too fast
Heroin makes you stupid and slow.

There are a million bands in the US
Five hundred thousand of them are better than you guys
Loaded, trashed, miss the changes
Forget lyrics
Late for practice, hassled and broke.
Running out of beer, low on dope
Play in a dark basement
You miss out on
Weekends, full paychecks, a happy home
Good sex, dependable transportation
Miss out on nothing
Loud, fast and hard
A fair trade.

Track 2. Guitar Players in Trouble (Prog Rock)

Both were good musicians, neither to be trusted.
Lead was thoughtful, a little weird
Shifty
He listened to string quartets and Surf Music
Built long solos from fragments of both
Teutonic and dense
On a seafoam green Stratocaster
The threat of a dark sky above
Perfect waves, seductive, smooth, deep.

The uncluttered
Rhythm smiled too often, distracted
But had stamina to pile chords, supportive, strung out
Spiraling melodies
Couldn't drink much before he nodded off to sleep
They had a ball
Everyone but Rhythm's wife
Home with the baby
Made her own clothes
Cooked with all natural ingredients
Small, dark, calm, a writer of fantasy stories
She sang a few songs in a wavering alto
She was good, more folk than rock
But welcomed by the band

Feminized the guys
Until she slept with the lead guitar, him,
That sneaky bastard
It all went to hell.

On the way home from practice
A rainy night, crap car, beer drunk and weed
The lead guitar tells the drummer
Out of nowhere, softly, slipped in like a new phrase in
An old tune "I had sex with Helen. A lot. For a few months. She's
very active. More than you would think."
The drummer driving.
Which is never a good idea
And he pulls the wheel hard to the left to stay on the slick
Unlit road
Shocked
And jealous
Knows another band is finished
It's over, the breakup, the fadeout.
Try to end the song at the same time.

    Track 3. Boom boom Gets Arrested (Long Psychedelic Surf Fuzz Reverb)

Bass player
Under indictment
Short of money crashes on a friend's couch.
Boom boom has played bass
Since he was 12
The tallest in his class
The amount of dope he smokes
Is impressive and when the tune begins
He can't remember his part
Depends on the drummer,
Guitars, anyone, to please remind him
What he played last time.

When he gets in the groove

He'll be just fine, fine,
Bopping on the thick strings with conviction.
Doesn't take anything seriously
Except pot or the back end
Of a twelve pack never passes up a line of blow
Deals some because he can't make a living playing bass and
When he was arrested he missed practice
Due to meetings with his lawyer
Pawned his guitar every week
Make a payment, stay out of jail
Stretch out that song with a plea bargain
The band has to dig down
Pool their cash, bail out the bass,
Drop by the hock shop on the way to a gig
A pain in the ass, Boomboom,
But what else to do? He wasted time, cost money
But he was the bass player.

Have to be loyal to your bass player.

Track 4. Drum Brain (Hard Blues with Required Drum Solo)

Drummer in back, against a wall, in the dark
Let guitars take the heat

Stoned to the teeth,
Watches rock&roll calligraphy ripple off his cymbals
(Loves his cymbals)
Red-eye pinpoint light on the bass amp steady
Steady
Tripping rhythm
Kicking in the beat
Crashing brass
Paradiddles and
Doublestroke rolls
Kicking ass (Drop a stick)
Oh goddamnit
Tight-tuned snare with enough

Give and bounce and tension to lay deep into the groove.
All he needs is a tight well-tuned snare
Time, meter, tempo
No one is looking and he thinks, "It's all I need."

Track 5. The Singer (Angry Punk Rip-off With Vomit)
Where is the singer? It's time

We have to move equipment
Set up the amps, position mics
Arrange the drumset, anchor the band
Check the set list, revise lyrics
Someone has to stand at the rear of the
Bar
Hall
Club
Studio
Gymnasium
Picnic area
Listen for balance
And make decisions
Supposed to be a group effort, turn up
Turn down, more echo, play quieter, can't hear lyrics.

Where the hell is the singer?
The drummer is going to kick the singer's ass
One of these days
That's a promise they see it coming
Play together for years
And the singer is still late, shows up empty-handed with a big grin
Hits the bar
Orders his drink
Chats the waitress.

Where in the goddamn hell is the singer?
The bass player has a big amp, he's high and
Needs help getting up on stage without hurting himself
Again

Drums require six or seven trips
The drummer is exhausted, sweating before the first note
Guitars noodle until the last
Possible moment never satisfied
And the singer is in the toilet with the cocktail waitress
Another line of blow, licks it off her upper lip
Slams a couple of shots
Scribbles a phone number on a wet napkin
Grin kiss preen.

Where is the singer?
Is he driving around the block looking for the best parking place?
Scoring off one of those sleazy creeps at the bar? Yukking it up with the bartender?
The drummer is tired, half drunk and has had it
Up to here
With the goddamn singer.
"That's it. I am going to find him and kick his ass.
we can play instrumentals for the rest of our lives. He's never lifted
A finger to move a piece of equipment and gets a
Fair share, an even cut from the tip jar, tells everyone he's
In a band, is a lazy, well-dressed poser with
Friends, people love him, he has a decent day job
And that is it, it's over, I'm going to kick his ass." "Where is he? Where is the goddamn singer?"

Track 6. Bottom of My Glass (Country Derivative, Merle Haggard, George Jones)

Graduation rolled around
I was nowhere to be found
I was drunk and blacked out in a coma

Didn't study history
Math was a mystery
Never bothered to pick up my diploma

I graduated at the bottom of my glass
My grades were bad, I knew I'd never pass
No books no friends no sports or history class
I graduated at the bottom of my glass

Started younger than I should
Drinking whiskey when I could
Cut school and slept out in the cold

My parents drank their dinner
Brother and I got thinner
I was nine when the impulse took hold

I'm not the fastest reader
Never been a natural leader
They said I had the lowest marks in school

Mom and dad would bicker
But I could hold my liquor
They didn't raise their boy to be a fool

I graduated at the bottom of my glass
My grades were bad I knew I'd never pass
No books no friends no sports or history class
I graduated at the bottom of my glass

Transient Back Pain

I hope it's temporary.
My back is killing me.

Not literally, but I'm dying.

I'm dying.
No worries about dying but this morning at 3 a.m.
I was awake for a half hour
Taking my pulse. Rapid.
Back pain or anxiety.
I'm dying and there is no one to tell me that I'm not dying
Because Sally really died and will never again say
 "You'll be OK soon; you are healthy; You have many, many years left."
What I hear is: It's all in your head, what's wrong with you, go outside,
Exercise, lose weight.

My back follows me like the years; my history is merciless.
My heart.
I lost ten pounds last month and my back improved
Then flared up again
Hellpain down my left leg from waist to heel
How the holy crap?
Admission: I have not taken the best care of myself.
In times of panic I've cleaned up, cut back on sweets
Conscientious about health, health food, healthy living
But most of my life I've disregarded signs, aches, advice,
And had another drink
A smoke
Coke
Adventures ended in injury
And now, excuse me for laughing,
I have back pain
My back is killing me.
The ten pounds I lost was a good idea, no doubt
 Plenty of advice from fellow sufferers: Lose weight and you'll feel better

That's true.
I feel better. Everywhere but in my back which is killing me
Another ten or fifteen pounds may help
Admission: I've been twenty or twenty-five pounds overweight for decades.
My doctor says I could lose thirty-five pounds
Get way down, down to
My teenage weight when I was vigorous and strong and
Vital
Miserable and wished I were dead every day.

My doctor, who scolded me every six months about my weight,
Died.
He had a disease and died and was a month younger than I.
I didn't laugh. I was smug. I ate too much that day
When I got the news. Good guy, my old doctor.
Now gone and I'm here
Right here
My back is killing me.

The new doctor is young, younger by thirty years.
He's skinny, handsome and has great hair
Tells me I could "afford" to lose weight.
I ignore his advice in the same way I ignored my old doctor's advice
Don't take suggestions, I nod and dismiss his instructions
Except for medications. I take meds. I ask for more. I get refills.
I'm good about drugs
I'm great about pain medication for my back.
OK. I'll do it
I'll work and exercise and diet and plan and eat better
And in a year I'll be down thirty, thirty-five pounds.
My back may stop killing me.
If not? I can always gain the weight back
Go deep into the fridge
Buy some cookbooks
Indian Food. Soups. Learn to make bread

Baked desserts. Cookies.

I walk for a while and the pain stops and then it kills me
Sitting, I feel relief. Then I stand up. Temporary. Everything is transitory.
My weight is variable
My pain sporadic
Writing is ephemeral
All temporary
Sally has died
Even
My doctor is temporary.

Breaking the Poetry Code

In the poems
Whenever you read "Soup"
Replace it with "Hand Job"

Where a reference to
Weather appears
Assume that I am writing about
Death.

Poetry is always Poetry unless
I modify the system this coming Thursday
(Thursday is when everything changes)
Then poetry is either
Theft, infidelity or remorse.
I don't write about love
And if I mention Pets, Plants or Children
I am referencing old movies, introversion and my inherent selfishness.
When you read "Haircut" Replace it with "Hand Job".

Enemy

How does he do that? How can he do that? How can he simply say that
   While wearing that hat?
   He makes his own shoes, I swear,
   They look ridiculous
   But why should I care? They're his feet, his shoes, his socks and
   He rarely wears socks
   How does he walk around looking like that?
   His grey skin testifies to decades of mishandled narcotics and
   Drink.

A face lined and leathery from lying on the ground
Pockmarks punctuate a blank look
Gray eyes are deep, small, and confused
He insulted me and he's the enemy
Against whom I plan revenge.

   Wait. Get a grip. He's older than me, has had a triple by-pass, a damaged
   Liver, face is hanging on by a thread, cholesterol incalculable
   Blood thick with diabetes, and he will drop like a stone in
   A few months, a year at most.

   But, goddamnit, he rides a bicycle.
   He has nothing, can't drive, no money
   No hope, no prospects, can't pay bills or buy things,
   Will settle for any kind of attention but the dick rides a bicycle.
   I don't ride a bike
   And he is my enemy.

   I haven't had an enemy in twenty years.
   Plenty to choose from, others,
   But they're not enemies. I turn the dial
   They dissolve. I've learned how to

Loosen my grip, say aloud, alone, "I don't care."
Murphy was a childhood enemy because he saw
Breasts before I did. Stupid reason to make an enemy

   Tony Monteverdi was going to "Ruin My Life" because I slept with his wife.
   I understand now, makes sense.

   Linda became an enemy due to the fact that I was married, lied and lied to her for years
      She said she'd call the cops if I ever contacted her
      She was right. I never called again
      Not an enemy
      A victim.

I Beat Cancer's Ass (For a Friend in Remission)

That kid, that woman, the handsome young man, hairless, smile too broad
Dark circles under their eyes
Hold up a sign, click, like and share if you hate cancer.
I beat cancer. I hate cancer.

Me, too. I hate cancer, too, I do,
(What's the alternative? Doesn't everyone hate cancer? Jeez.)

I called cancer
Invited cancer over to the house
Drugged it and when cancer awoke I kicked cancer's ass
When I was done beating cancer, it took a while,
Wore me out I had a smoke
Listened to cancer snivel and plead
Crying and drippy and bleeding
Turned cancer over my knee,
Spanked cancer until my hand was numb and cancer's butt blistered

Cancer begged
Afterwards, when cancer started to stink
From fear and sweat and blood and snot I kicked goddamn cancer out of the house
Didn't even give cancer its shoes
Ha, and I watched as cancer limped away
Gagging, broken
Septic
Incoherent jabbering
Pathetic
And then
When cancer was a few blocks up the street and thought it was safe
I got in my car and drove alongside forced cancer into the trunk
Took cancer back to my place
Dragged it through the kitchen

Threw cancer down the basement stairs
Began again

Cancer asked me to, please,
Kill it, such a filthy disease
I laughed and spit on cancer
Tied cancer to an overhead beam trussed like a chicken
The oncologist's dream
I'm going to humiliate, spit, curse and abuse cancer
  Until I can't stand the sight of it any more, no longer amused I'll let cancer hang there Suffer
  Until I get bored, I'll watch cancer bleed
On the basement floor
I film it all
You think you hate cancer?
Uh uh
I really hate cancer
More than you
I beat cancer's ass
Beat it bad

Get well soon I know you can
Love and light
Hugs
Lots of hugs.

Big Questions

Where did I come from Where am I going
Why am I blah, blah, blah?
Is there meaning to life,
Where were we before we were born? How long should I wait for someone who is late?
Is there a God in heaven? Is heaven on earth or in Iowa?
Aren't there too many styles of shoes?
Why do we dream and
What do they mean?
Do I talk in my sleep? What is mucous?
Why would a bird walk anywhere?
Quick, would you rather be rich or invisible?
Is this the beginning of the end or just the last episode of the first season?
Sleeping is a little death
And if death is eternal sleep why do I wake up on the floor?
How does metabolism engage
With the endocrine system to create anxiety and low self esteem?
Who named one way "right" and the other "left"?
Should we be punished for
Lying about sex?
Ask the universe a question. Why does the universe always answer, "You're too late?"
In a past life, in a different incarnation,
In another era, haven't we all been civil servants who are allergic to shellfish?
Angels, ghosts, specters
Immortal essence, eternal spirit and baboons.
Where did you come from
Where are you going
Why are you blah, blah, blah?

In the Shower

I do not trust myself to write love poetry

There are many reasons
if I needed only one
It would be this:

Mornings when I hear the shower door close with a snap
And water run on tile
Warming
I listen from bed
Before rising to stand
Silently, unmoving with caught breath

Simply listen
Splatter and splash
 I knock, polite if nothing else, I knock to hear her voice when she sings out in a sweet Accented foreign tone, a character she only plays
 As she soaps and stands under the spray
 "Come In. Entri, per favore, signore."

Completely and fully prepared for anything
No limits, come in
Come right in
And I
Entre and she is
Blurred by the fogged glass
Stands straight and presses against the
Steamed window
Her figure, skin and shadows, formless hands
Hazy at the end of long arms
She was unflawed
Ageless, steamy perfect warm and clean.

Tell Me

Sally Gray is gone.
When I told her she had ink on her cheek
When I pointed out that her blouse was buttoned wrong
When I said that her sleeve was in the butter
She became angry and embarrassed because
She was beautiful and accomplished and
Hated missteps.
To be brilliant for 74 years, to read the history
Of the French monarchy for pleasure
Did not allow for perceived insults
Offered with respect, love.
She spoke fluent French
Asked in in English
"Would you want me to tell you those things?"

Please,
Tell me if I have food in my teeth
If my breath is sour
Take me aside
Let me know
If my zipper is opened, if my fly is down
Please
Tell me and I'll sort it out, pull it up or leave it.
Tell me if the oven is on and you smell gas
Take chances
Tell me something you've never told anyone else
Trust me.

Recommend a good book but don't expect me to read it.
    Please don't give me a copy of the book
    Someday you'll ask for it and I'll spend an hour
    Looking through the shelves and
    End up buying a new copy because
    The one you leant me is moldy
    The cover has come off.

I have to know how deep is the water
If a car is coming towards us

If I drop my wallet, glasses, phone
If you see a snake
If I'm getting sunburned
Please tell me if someone says something nice
About me, complimentary, flattering
You're not here and I'm sad to say
I get most of my thin veneer of self-esteem
Externally
From others
I've never been able to generate it from within
It was the great gift you gave.

Tell me in a single, short, well-crafted sentence
What I missed in the film when
I went to the restroom.
That's a lesson we should all learn.

For parties, events, holidays
Tell me what time I should be there
Can I bring something?
I want to help, participate
Feel normal and neutral for once
I'd like to be welcomed back
I can make cookies
No problem, tell me what you'd like
I'll make cookies
I'll stand at the front door
Alone
Nervous, too early
With a smile and a plate of cookies.

Tell me if that guy at the end of the bar
Has been looking at me
Like he wants to kick my ass
Tell me if he stands up
Tell me if there are good tomatoes for sale
Mangos
Watermelon
Tell me if you see my doctor, dentist,
Therapist

Drunk
That would be good to know, right?
Tell me if you see a cop
If you understand the end of The Sopranos
Or Lost. What the hell was that about?

Tell me to pick up your meds
On my way home.

I took cookies to a party and no one ate them.

There are those who tell me that they only fly first class
They own two houses
They wear a Rolex
They tell me about God, UFOs, Astrology, Tarot
Their IQ
The value of the house
Their trip to India
Their spiritual awakening
How much they meditate
How to pronounce "Quinoa"
Their BMI
Their kids are gifted.

You never told me those things.
Thank you.

You didn't brag or boast
Nor did you swagger and pose
There was no pretense
At times I had to pry
Early days you told me you were bipolar
You were well modulated, unnoticeable
Until I found the hidden suicide notes
Not manifested, mood disorder, but my God
You should have told me
When I found out, I did my best, helped I think, I worked so hard
You became settled, well,
Near perfect.

Wonderfully well.

How come no one told me,
That you were going burst a
Goddamn aneurysm
While swimming in the municipal pool
On April 6
And die?
I could have used that information.
Helpless.

Now you can't tell me
Anything
Ever

Oh, goddamnit, someone tell me why
You were the only person who ate my cookies
My own recipe
You asked to eat the leftover dough
It says right on the package of flour that
Raw dough
Can cause illness
I handed you the bowl and said,
"Here you go. Feeling lucky?"
We laughed at that
We laughed…

No one told me that it would be the last time
No one else cared about the cookies
Thanks for telling me you loved me and believing.
For being nice to me. You may have been the first.

Tell me
Please tell me
How to do this
Without you
How to be without, without everything
Without.

Brave Oyster

Brave oyster burrowed in the sand
With limited perceptions you're nothing but a gland

You don't have a leg; you're missing either hand
Deep in the frigid ocean, far from solid land

A filter on the bottom of a dirty oily sea
Sucking in water and spitting out pee

Another wave of crap to fill your heart with glee
Garbage filth and poison satisfy your needs

Solitary, you slide along the bottom all alone
Don't know where you're going, nowhere to call home

No sex no talk no fun no friends no skin no funny bone
Don't know if you're in the Arctic or the Torrid Zone

But wait, brave oyster, what's that pain deep inside your shell?
A bit of sand has lodged in your tissues and your jell

A pearl will bud and grow and torment your days
The throbbing stinging misery for which a sucker pays

To string them on a cord of twine and hang them round a neck
Something that you will never comprehend

The taste and touch of skin
Sad asexual oyster with not a chance to sin

Brave oyster in the sand
Joke of an idiot god
You feast on second helpings of muck and crud
You'll never have an oyster Eve to motivate your blood
To beckon you to lie with her, naked in the mud

When I'm alone in misery and wish that I were dead
Discouraged, pissed and bored, horrors of my head

I think of you, brave oyster, in your gritty dirty bed

You gloomy aching dripping, snotty
Unloved ignored effluvium-drunk
Rubbish-munching bottom dwelling
Peasant
Of the unfathomable abyss.

Some Poems Should Never

A desire to write
To front myself to anyone who'll read

Cringing memory of a poem that never should have been.
I struggled with the form, a villanelle (I remember),
Drink wine all night
Fit the
Pieces together.
Alas.
The rhymes were stretched to snapping
Bands and locks and blocks of sound to grip the stanza tight
Content and meaning paid a price.
Meter was easier in those days; I had rhythm and I could dance
(Note: I enjoyed the dance. My partner and I, drunk, weave and caress
To bluesy songs in a long gone bar, to the wise cracks, laughter,
Aroma of weed, sound of ice and arguments
Time slowed because there was dance.)

The pencil tips across the page as day breaks
The villanelle is complete.
(Note: This nineteen-line poem has only two rhymes throughout but also
Involves five tercets with a goddamn quatrain,
And, get this; the first and third lines of the opening tercet repeat
Alternately at the (oh god) end of the other tercets
Both repeated at the conclusion of the final quatrain.)

I read it.
To people. Students. A professor. A dark place. I knew before I was halfway that it was Shit.
Dry mouth
Hands tremble (I heard the poem stutter).
If I could remember the title I'd tell, but it is gone.

May have been a nature poem.
Or death. I knew little of nature and not enough of death.

So bad, villanelle with its crafty lines and rhymes, jiggling and yattering
On the quivering page.
Comments? Oh yes. One. A thin young man stands, looks directly at
Me, says the thing I will never forget: "Some poems should never have been written."
Silence follows; the silence was an endorsement of his judgment.

I sniffed and gave the illusion of thought; head down, inch towards my seat
Thought: Bite me. That can't be true. Can it? Might have been a bad poem but
What the hell? Have to write something.
Never again a villanelle.

Bedtime Story

 Mommy and Daddy are getting a divorce and it's all your fault
 We were happy at first, for a few years,
 Now we are not and that's because of you
 You will live with Mommy sometimes and Daddy on weekends
 But we will never be together because
 We are tired and angry and we
 Stopped loving each other. Which doesn't mean we don't love you
 No, no It just means we love you less than we did when we were
 Together and pretending.

 Remember when we went to the lake that week and laughed
 And had so much fun and you learned to hold your breath and
 Put your face in the water?

 We'll never do that again because
 We're splitting up we will try to make you comfortable; you may have your own bed
 But not for a while and not if you don't do what we say
 If you don't do what you are told
 You will then live with other people
 We don't know who they are
 But if you are not quiet, good, you will have to
 Live with them and you may never see us again.

 These things happen and now this has happened to us
 Never forget that it's your fault I'm sorry if it hurts
 How do you think we feel? Now we have to separate and we will do our best
 But we are angry and the future looks
 Dark. Cold. Lonely. Sad.
 That's because of you
 You won't see your friends.
 You can make new friends.

There will be no room and we will give away your toys and most of your clothing
We won't be able to stay in our house, we will have to move

Mommy and Daddy will live in small rooms and you'll sleep on the couch
Or the floor. When you hear Mommy and Daddy fighting it is your fault
Something you did.
We want
We want to be happy, is all we want
Now go to sleep
We'll talk more in the morning.

Secrets to Success Part I

Low Expectations. Yes.

The Secret. Low Expectations obtained by
Managing disappointment. You have to do it on your own
Who the hell teaches
Low Expectations? What school has "Expectations 101: Low" on the
Schedule this fall?

Take chances, ask inappropriate questions, write
A short story, sign up for open mike,
When there is no applause, no praise
Estimate the level of sadness
Rage, self-hate that develops then
Divide by the silence of failure (A ringing in the ear, a pulsatile whine
That subsides with indifference.)
That's all you need:
Low Expectations.
And a good haircut.

Secrets to Success Part II

During our last discussion I thought we all agreed that the road to success
Is paved
With lowered expectations and a good haircut.

Many disputed this. Some were angry, others hurt.
"Prayer was never mentioned", moaned a scold
From San Jose.
"What about a shoe shine"? asked a waiter from Las Vegas.
"The Golden Rule was not on your list", reminded an
Isolated busybody.
"A haircut is fine but you can't put a price on
good oral hygiene", opined
A recovered wino named Faustino.

What can I say to those who won't listen
Or reject change,
Who refuses to believe, are unwilling to
Accept truth, how do I tell them
Why they are wrong
And what they can do to improve?

Here's an exercise:
Pronounce the word "Failure" aloud. Sound it out. Do it.
Emphasize each letter, exhale on the last syllable and hold
Say it (failure) again and again (failure) until it becomes strange, foreign.

Failure
Loses its significance.
Do this for an hour every day.
Lower expectations and a good haircut. No more questions.

Zeus Rebukes A Minor God

You cannot have the storm
I am taking it back
I thought you could handle the storm
But you cannot
It is obvious
You cannot manage aggravated weather
When belligerence and passion are needed

During your last review you were warned to get it together
Concentrate
Learn a few basic laws of science
But you are lazy
Thought you could control the storm and no one would notice

Obvious errors:
The rain.
What were you thinking?
Your rain wasn't even close to correct; it fell sporadically,
The odd cloudburst
It was an embarrassment to the storm
Not enough to cause deadly flooding in the suburbs
Your pissing drippy sputter of rain
Sad
You are finished with the storm
And the wind? Holy God
The wind is supposed to howl, blow rain sideways
Topple trees, rip the siding off of houses, umbrellas
Inside out, hats long gone, dresses flipped up and shirts undone
The wind was awkward to say the least
The breeze, the steady caress that one longs for in summer a serious misstep
What we need during a storm is a rough ragged ruinous gale of
Unrestricted madness and danger, strong enough to
Lock kids indoors
Take the wheel of the car and turn towards the railing

As they drive across the bridge
Damn, now that's a wind.

You cannot handle the storm. What about clouds? How could anyone consider that Vaporous crap hanging up there Cloud?
Your tragic clouds show that you are unclear on the notion of abstraction.
It was not worth the effort
Storm clouds are dark, thick In the center and bighearted gray massive
Endless and foreboding
Plunging across the expanse to obscure any
Hope that there may be sky above.

As long as we are on the subject of clouds What the hell is this
Deceit with the illusion of silver lining?
Who gave you permission? Why would you do that? Overhead sinister stormclouds Every once in a while there appears to be a light framing
The menace;
Nice try but you are a failure, a fraud
Silver linings are deception, the enormous delusion of the Inexperienced.

You thought I wouldn't notice
I've been at this so much longer than you
You're done here
Get your things and get out of my sight before I call security
You lose. You cannot have the storm.

The Denunciation of St. Peter

St. Peter dipped in his own blood and left to dry
Under the white sky
Heat unbearable
He strains at straps across his burned chest
Wiggles caked fingers

There is nothing to breathe but his own filth

Laughing soldiers rest on their spears
And toss fresh goat dung at his face
He shakes his head, a small turd drops into his mouth

If it can happen to St. Peter, it can happen to anyone.

Diabetes II – An Affirmation

Stay away from sugar
Stay away from sweet
Get diabetes
They cut off your feet

Don't eat flour
Don't eat pie
Delicious desserts
Make you die

Your skin will peel
Your tongue will swell
There's no Haagen-Dazs in hell

Diabetic coma insulin OD
You'll go blind
It'll hurt to pee

Eat some candy
Drink a coke

Have a donut
Have a stroke

Titles for Unwritten Poems

The Tarzan Outbreak
Genetically Predisposed to be Alone (A Fantasy in three parts)
You May Win But That Doesn't Mean You're Right
I Blame Myself but I Blame You More
The Misguided Mentor of Mendocino
Forget it, You'll Be Better Off
Climbing the Wrong Tree
These Are Your New Feet
Clambake in Sector 14
Scary Days Ahead (A Children's Story)
River of Filth: Part 3
You Have a Hole In Your Pajamas
Sorry She Was Ever Born
His New Toaster

Did You Hear Something?
It's just the house settling.
What do you mean, the house settling? We've lived here for 15 years. Shouldn't the house have settled by now. I think there's someone in the yard. Go and see. Take the Flashlight.

I don't know where the flashlight is.

Goddamn you're helpless. It's in the drawer next to the stove.
It's always in the drawer next to the stove. In the Kitchen.

Help me look for it.

OK, I'll help you find it, but this house is not settling.
I swear, there's someone out there.

Waste of time. I have to get up early.
Well, you won't have to worry about getting up
When you've been murdered in your bed. You won't have to set the alarm when you're dead. Christ almighty, the house is not settling.

Dropping the E

My handwriting has degenerated. There is a pinched nerve
In my neck and the fingers of my right hand become numb.

I revise and examine the page and discover
That I have dropped the letter E at the end of words such as Home and Love?

My lack of E may be a result of hardened arteries, cognitive
Degeneration, sloppy penmanship, psychic disorder, pain medication.
I simply forget to write the concluding E on words that can be
Pronounced and understood clearly without the added burden
Of the final silent E that is confusing and unnecessary.

How do we expect anyone to learn this language?
"No, no, Carmine, it's Shame, not Shamay. Shame, Shame.
Not Blamay, but Blame. I know it's confusing but we're Americans.
It's what we do."

If it is silent it is probably superfluous. My eviction of the E is,
Maybe, a form of unconscious modernization, an evolution in writing.
A rebel puts a jot, a mark at the intersection of two letters
Thus creating the conjunctions. Don't, Can't, Won't.

A line of code that makes life easier, less rigid for speakers and writers.
Thank you to those victims of the literary Inquisition,
Wardens took one look at the first official document that included an
Apostrophe, grunted, squinted, hissed, and arrested the writer for a round of
Torture, a bit of the rack, some branding, until they re-

nounce the apostrophe
   Deny the demonic modification, an insult to accepted belief.

   Am I the reincarnation of the he who boldly
   Spit an apostrophe in the face of the pope, the judge, the Minister of Standards?
   Can I convince my readers, the few, the disenchanted, despairing and
   Corrupt, can I sell them the concept that I drop the E with dignity?

   There are many linguistic sidetracks, but the silent E, for God's sake
   The damned E? It is overused, no doubt, but we've become so familiar
   With it. It is in every commonly written email, text, suicide note.
   Is unconscious suppression of the letter E significant or just slovenly?

   I'm not daring enough to completely eliminate the silent E from my work.
   Fate would be fat; Love looks so small while hate becomes a hat.
   I wondered at first, why am I doing this, dropping this E, why does the line
   Look smaller, still makes sense, but now the words are constricted and
   I don't want to be responsible for that. For reducing the language
   For eliminating anything. I'm not that confident.

   The E remains
   And I will commit to carefully pressing it into the space allotted
   Whether it expands meaning or not. Who do I think I am, the
   Grand Arbiter of E, the Tsar of the Common Vowel, Master of Truncation?

Am I merely repressing my incipient fear of the banal? It's only an
E. Not some world-changing amendment to space, time, light and sound.
I am mortal. The E is not. It will continue, long after I'm gone and forgotten.

I'm sad. I write about the eternity of the letter E and I become sad.
What next? First the E, then the elimination of
Homonyms, such as their, they're and there, which has begun in our time.
I will be gone and the letter E will live on, enduring even
To the End of Days, the E will be the last remaining letter on our failed globe.
Globe without the E would be Glob and all my poems are about death.

In Vitro

Headline:72-Year-Old Woman in India Gives Birth to a Boy
(May 13, 2016)

What a terrific idea
Fertilize human eggs outside of the body
I love this world
Love the eggs
Gooey and thick
In a petri dish
In a coffee cup
In a bird feeder

In a laboratory where they grow strong and violent
What a terrific idea (Daddy spilled beer on the last batch
Didn't tell anyone until it was too late
Excused himself, said, "I'm going out to get cigarettes.")
No Daddy, no more, not needed, a problem daddy
In Vitro will fill the world with kids free from
The Father.
Mother, too, is also redundant.

Yes, finally. Embryos like salmon roe slipping around
In an ashtray, sputtering their rejection of desire
Desire obsolete, as outmoded as parents.
Mother's day, an historic memory resembling Armistice Day.

There are too many cords to cut, the scissors are dull
And we're running out of towels.
The nurse turns, drops a basin full of instruments, shouts,
"Oh shit the canal is clogged with the bodies of the unborn."

No seed will go to waste
The uterus folds in on itself, at rest while all penises go on
Vacation
Yet, a world bursts with fertility
Swollen and sticky
Can I hold it? You have so many. Can I hold just one of them?

Priest

Warming up in mid-morning
Lean against the pink stucco wall
Of the liquor store.
Poorly painted mural beckons
Amuses patrons with a postcard image of an island
Gentle waves break on white sand
Palm trees bend elegantly to the sky
Surf rolls a full bottle of rum
Onto the beach, back again to the sea
Soon it will be above the waterline
To be discovered.

It is early and few customers
Shop for drink in daylight
The door swings open
The priest, shiny black suit, white collar. He nods, a bottle in a bag
Held close
He has a broken nose
I have one of those.
"How'd you break your nose, Father?"
"Rugby years ago. And you?"
"One fight and one foul ball. I was waiting to
get up to bat."

He laughs and tells his parable of the broken nose
Made sure I understood; his job
To help, to do good.

"Don't bother getting it fixed, unbent
even if you can afford it. Mine was repaired
a decade ago. Eggshell bones crushed
reset to allow airflow for the
first time in memory
and it was glorious, a miracle to
deeply draw the breath and feel It flow
No difficulty, in, out, air, the
smartest thing I'd ever done.

Why did I wait so long?

I held my head high, tasted the crisp
bite and rush of health filling my lungs
and was young again.
For six months I breathed like an athlete
considered taking up golf, sailing, basketball
equal on the court
to the young and intact, youthful memories
ran in my blood along with a generous measure of oxygen.
Six months of effortless inhalation, vigor,
but hope receded, drifted away
as this nose
repositioned itself, renewed the pre-surgical
architecture, narrowed, and once again I gasped
through my mouth
simply to stay alive. Shit. I'd been impaired for
so long, crooked, damaged, blocked that
the promise of reparation
took me full on, filled me with confidence.
Wrong. Again wrong.
Once the damage is done you have to live with it.
It cannot be altered, no matter what
   penance, amends, atonement, contrition, mortification, surgery.

I am worse than before. I awake panicked
unable to satisfy my lungs, once awake I am sorry for everything.
The promises they make to recreate you
as a healthy and fully oxygenated man
are false. Words.
Live with your deformities.

You breath with difficulty? Yes. As do I.
As do we all. Change Is painful and expensive. Have a drink.
try the Rum."

He stepped back, looked at the mural on
The pink stucco wall, inhaled, a quiet whistle, a sigh.

Her Ray Gun

On fresh paved gentle highway 160 Between Durango and Pagosa Springs
Through dark pine forest, mountains out there, everywhere in the distance
Clouds come in to own it all
Pumped full with rain.

Sweet air from an open window
And a small silver beast-car BMW or Audi or Porsche
Fast, too fast, darts from behind from nowhere
Rips the road, flings up rocks and dust, passes with a mocking high-pitched horn blast
Snarls, slips off edge of the world
Maneuvers to the center line smears the scenery
Arrows into a quick distance.

Asshole

She, in the passenger seat, rests her head, enjoys the view
Says, "I wish I had a ray gun to zap that guy."

"Me, too, for sure, a weapon to crash his car and set it on fire
so I can pull up, get out and stand over him, piss on him as he burns to death, an hour of agony, while
I spit curses and insults, watch him turn a painful glowing ash
sputtering fat, broken teeth
A cracked blistered skull.
Yes."

"No. I don't want to kill him. Just make him disappear so that
we can drive without disturbance. No suffering."

Oh. OK. OK. I misunderstood
The nature of your ray gun.

The Last Supper

The last supper, the last flirtation, the last automobile, the last cat,
The last supper, the last rash, the last coffee, the last great book,
The last supper, the last love, the last donut,
The last supper, the last cigarette, the last virus, the last of Kurosawa,
The last supper, the last load of wash, the last dental appointment,
The last supper, the last bar of soap, The last supper, the last sad day,
The last tears, finally,
The last broken heart,
The very last supper.

Why Am I Standing in This Line?

Room I'm in a room.
Line, I've been standing in line a long line with strangers
It's night now
The sun is down and I cannot see the front of the
Line.
Room
In a room.
Dark, the room is dark and I cannot see into the corners
Door
The door is closed
Straight backed chair at a table with a dim lamp
Paper
Blank paper
A pen,
There is a pen on the table. Pick it up
Fit it to the hand
And write.
 "Why was I standing in line? What were we Waiting for? Where did they go? What Room"? What is expected?'
 Am I supposed to Write? There is nothing else to do.
The door closes silently.

Tuesdays

9 a.m. (Coffee)
Sally discovered the croissants and took me there for the great pastry.
Good coffee. She knew people in coffee shops on four continents. In Paris I stayed home to write each morning while she explored the neighborhood. She found Le Voltigeur in the Marais, met Patrice the waiter, we spent Christmas in his tiny apartment with his generous friends. The weird swag lamps and fluorescent colors of Le Perpiniere were to her taste. Her wonderful light sophisticated French helped and the staff was happy to see us, welcomed us back.
Sally introduced me to owners, bartenders, waiters. They liked her. I stood distant to convey benevolence without being approachable. I was not as bold as Sally. When Sally died I was startled by global messages of support.
"Hey, Joe, how are you doing? So sorry, man."
Hugs and handshakes and sincere expressions of concern.
Today, alone, when I ordered my plain croissant, the owner said, "They're pretty small this morning. I'll give you two."
"Thanks a lot. My goal weight is 300 pounds."
She laughed, I took my two croissants and small coffee to a table outside, set up my computer, plugged in my earphones and tried not to weep.
Fabulous croissants. Should I pretend? Stay home? Change coffee shops? There is no escape.

11 a.m. (Therapy)
I'm never late for my appointment. My therapist is also named Sally and was Sally Gray's therapist. Awkward coincidence.
Therapist Sally wears a tiny stud in her nose. Her hair is impressive. Long chestnut locks in spiraling curls. A sparkle. Three glistening strands of tinsel woven into her hair. A hint of gold. They cost a dollar apiece at her hairdresser's. I asked. We have that relationship. I admire her refined vivacity and uncanny intuition.
At times a single spark catches the sun as she turns her head to consider my desolation. A bright punctuation to a

dark hour.

Noon (Shopping for one)
I've nodded to the guy at the market several times a week for the past ten years. He's a senior employee, a nice looking, heavyset Hispanic man, outgoing. He greets me, "Good morning, amigo."
I asked for some tobacco. Skimmed the packet across the scanner, a notice appears with the message instructing me to call a customer service representative to see my ID. Cool.
I roll cigarettes, lumpy and loose, step out on the patio and light up. I started with half a cigarette three days a week and now I'm smoking many more. That's what happens. I've become powerfully addicted to any diversion from loss. I am dizzy and disoriented when I smoke but in time I'll, perhaps, be able to enjoy a cigarette and look at the stars. Both of those are difficult. The cigarette makes me sick; the stars nearly kill me.
The nice guy comes over, looks at me, laughs, says, "You have to be eighteen to buy tobacco, amigo."
"Yeah, I've learned that."

He waves a card on a lanyard around his neck and the machine emits the compliant tone that allows legal purchase of tobacco products.

"You roll your own?" he asks.
"Yeah, I've started smoking again. Rolling helps to keep it controllable."
"Really, man? You quit? How long ago?"
"Twenty-five years."
"Jesus, you must be under some stress."
"My wife died and I'll do anything, you know, for distraction."
His face changes, he puts his arm around my shoulder. "Lo siento. I am so sorry. Brother, what a drag."
"Yep. Thanks. Big pain everywhere but what can I do? I smoke."
"You take care, now."
"What else? Thanks. Adios."

7:30 p.m. (No doubt, worst of the day)

I sit in one of the weatherworn chairs on the patio in the evenings.
It's difficult to concentrate and few things interest me. The world is grey with variations. I was never good at identifying distinctions in color.
Blue sky, the earth dirty brown.
Sunflowers yellow and sunsets orange. Green grass, red blood, white snow.
Sally Gray knew more about art and color than anyone I've ever met.
Her education was extensive and admirable.
A local artist told me that she thought Sally's knowledge and appreciation of color
was at the most extraordinary, sophisticated and deep.
A nice thing to say; I was touched and proud.
At sunset I look up, unhappy, lonely, and the sky is not merely orange.
I rummage into my blurry brain to remember what color Sally would have seen.
Peach.
Holy Christ, the clouds are peach.
The sky is no longer merely blue.
I identify a touch of the palest green on humid days.
Soft rose on a cloudless twilight.

I have a red shirt but there is a slight shade of indigo,
It's compatible with my skin tone.
She said so.
I'll never wear yellow.
Something bad happens with yellow.
Yellow was her favorite color.
Under Sally's care, I can see colors, diverse and subtle things, alive.
For a quarter of a century life was exciting and full of surprises.
During that time I became her student of sensation, of revelations and grandeur.
I am different. Not better, but there is color.

CPSIA information can be obtained
at www.ICGtesting.com
Printed in the USA
BVHW040747160621
609642BV00008B/2048